The death of my husband that hot day in August forced me to take a road I would give much not to have needed to walk. Left with two young children and my shattered dreams, I tried courageously to be strong. But the path of grief was so painful and the emotional struggle so great that I wasn't sure I could cope with Rog's death.

Giving up the dreams I had shared with Rog seemed so impossibly hard, so intolerably sad. But I knew that only by stopping the past from overwhelming the present could I have any hope for the future.

My love for Rog and the beautiful memories will always be a special part of my life. The deep feelings that have turned to memories are there to recall and to build upon. But the past must be kept in its proper perspective — not an obsession, not a bondage — a good thing, but not the only thing.

I share my walk through grief, hoping that the grief process and the problems of being alone will be better understood by those who read this book — whether you are going through your own grief or standing by to help those who are bereaved.

# My Walk Through Grief

**Janette Klopfenstein**

Introduction by
**Bea Decker**
**Executive Director, Theos Foundation**

CHOICE
BOOKS

Published by Herald Press, a division of Mennonite
Publishing House, for Mennonite Broadcasts, Inc.

MY WALK THROUGH GRIEF
A Choice Book
Published by Herald Press, a division of Mennonite Publishing
House, for Mennonite Broadcasts, Inc.
Copyright © 1976 by Herald Press, Scottdale, Pa. 15683
Library of Congress Catalog Card Number: 76-3931
International Standard Book Number: 0-8361-1799-9.
Printed in the United States of America
Design by Alice B. Shetler

Second Choice Books edition, 1977

Choice Books are distributed by Mennonite Broadcasts, Inc.,
Harrisonburg, Va 22801. The word "Choice" and corresponding
symbol are registered in the United States Patent Office.

To those who helped me
through my walk
and to my sons,
Chad and Dereck,
who have kept life
interesting.

# CONTENTS

# INTRODUCTION

This book is a true story born from tragedy of an untimely death of a young father and husband. It is one young widow's walk through grief, from the moment she first learns of her husband's fatal disease. She struggles with the difficult questions of why God can permit a young husband and father, so good and full of ambition and love of life, to be struck by an uncurable illness and slowly lose his vitality and strength till in death he leaves his adoring wife and young sons.

An inspiring book, written directly from the heart, she shares her emotions in beautiful simplicity of how she was able to cope with a broken spirit and heart; but, through it all she is continually able to draw from a spiritual reserve greater than she had imagined.

Through her extraordinary talent to express her feelings on paper, Janette Klopfenstein shares with others who feel so alone, and with those who find it difficult to relate to anyone who has not experienced the loss of a beloved mate.

From her experience she offers sound and inspiring help for those in the throes of grief. She also offers practical advice to those friends and loved ones who truly want to help and understand the newly widowed.

*Bea Decker*, Coauthor
*After the Flowers Have Gone*

# PREFACE

Through the experience of Rog's death, I have learned that crisis can bring terrible pain and great struggle — and surprising bits of victory. Letting go of a person we love cannot be done quickly. Grief is a slow, hard walk. To rush through and avoid facing grief only provide a surface remedy.

In the process of my recovery, I have found some healing in being able to share with others. Many persons have encouraged me to put my thoughts into writing — in a kind of helping book for those going through the heartbreak of losing someone in death and for those standing by trying to help them put life back together again.

Instead of the typical "all things work together for good" kind of book, I attempt to show some of the raw emotions and terrible conflicts that people — including Christians — have to accept in facing death. Working through the situation and coming out on top of it to care deeply again about the quality of life involves a lot of personal pain. Believing in God does not take away all our difficulties, but through it all there is a quiet reassurance that He stands by.

I have tried to be practical in my suggestions and honest in expressing how it really feels to find oneself suddenly alone. Since I am a mother, I include much concerning young children.

I know I take the chance of appearing "too

confident" to the widowed and at the same time "too undone by my feelings" to those who haven't experienced the death of a loved one.

The book was written fifteen months after Rog's death — soon enough that the emotional struggles were still vivid in my mind but long enough after the death to give me a bit of perspective.

A special thanks to Mary Ann Miller, my support; Carolyn Sauder, my encouragement; Ellis Croyle, my best critic; Julie Nafziger, my typist; and to all those many others who have helped in my experience of sharing through this book.

*Janette Klopfenstein*
Archbold, Ohio

# MY GROWING
# APPREHENSION

Tears burned my eyes as I stood in the gigantic swimming pool watching the young father tossing the ball to his little girl as his smiling wife glowed with satisfaction. In a splash of water that echoed with fun, the father swam and ducked both of them. As they came sputtering to the top, their laughing eyes caught mine. I quickly turned away so the tears running down my cheeks wouldn't give me away.

The hollow feeling was there again. Everytime I saw a family running, tussling, and just physically enjoying each other, I felt the emptiness creep into my stomach. Muscular dystrophy, that ugly, incurable disease in which muscles of the body deteriorate, was robbing me of my ideal life. At twenty-nine, I deserved a husband who could swim, play sports, and be active with me. Chad, almost seven, and Dereck, almost four, needed a father who could tussle on the floor and toss football with them.

Instead we were 400 miles from our Archbold, Ohio, home visiting a clinic where Rog was receiving treatment for severe headaches which had plagued him for a year. Six months before he would have been enjoying the pool with us. Often now he was too exhausted and weak to join us in much physical activity. With haunting fear, I pictured a future with the possibility of a husband forced to accept the awful incapacity that the disease could bring.

I swam into the water to wash away the tears and shook the water from my face as I had so often recently shook off the panic that seemed to engulf me. The fact that Rog was still walking and that he still seemed in good health dispelled my self-pity about our lately-imposed nonathletic life.

Then, as I had done so frequently in the past four years since we heard those awful words, "Your weakness is a rare form of muscular dystrophy," I conjured up as much hope as I could and feverishly thanked God that I had a husband whom I loved dearly. "Oh, God, just keep him like he is. Don't let him get worse! We can live with his weakness."

16

Yes, we could live happily. Rog was so optimistic about life that his handicap of muscle weakness only served to make him a stronger, more positive person. He had spent a lifetime compensating for his condition and camouflaging it so well that many people were unaware he had a problem.

"Life is so good for us now. Just let it continue!" Our marriage, begun nine years before, had united two very different personalities. Rog was a quiet, steady person who knew what he wanted — a business career and a family. I was an outgoing, unsettled girl who wanted a teaching profession and worried that marriage would mean dishes, diapers, and stifled talent. Our three-year off-and-on dating ended with marriage when I realized that Rog's love and total acceptance of me was a rare thing — something I desperately wanted.

Instead of being stifled, I found that contentment in my personal life and the security of Rog's love left me free to develop in many areas. Rog worked as an accountant in a manufacturing business, while I finished college and then taught in a local high school. Our first small apartment was furnished with second-hand items. There was little money, but we thought we had it made.

With unusual good fortune, Rog moved up to assistant manager at age twenty-two and was caught up in the challenge of the business world. My pregnancy was welcomed by both of us and drew us closer than we thought possible. Our baby, Chad, not only arrived two months prematurely but also developed pneumonia. His successful battle for life against great odds made us thankful to God and extremely aware of the importance of family life.

The next years brought unusual happiness — our miracle child growing into a quick, happy little boy; our first home, an old frame one that we remodeled and decorated; a growing business which offered enjoyable fringe benefits, such as trips with wife included; part-time teaching for me; involvement in leadership at church; nurturing valued friendships; and then another child, our lively, dark-haired, beautiful-eyed Dereck.

When we learned that Rog's weakness — of which I was only slightly aware — was muscular dystrophy, we were stunned. "There is nothing to do about the disease. We can only check you every two years to determine your rate of deterioration," the university hospital specialist said. He indicated that the disease had likely started at birth and progressed very slowly. He advised that the decline in strength would probably continue to be gradual. "You may eventually need a cane and later perhaps a wheelchair," he said.

At times, we took the disease very seriously. We wrote to the Muscular Dystrophy Association offering to be guinea pigs for any new treatment and we received a nice reply saying they had nothing to offer. We tried Vitamin E and a moderate exercise program to keep strong the muscles that remained. We continually bumped against a medical world who told us nothing would help. Rog vacillated between short periods of serious searching for answers to the reasons for his deterioration and long periods of minimizing the disease so much that I thought it didn't really bother him. "I've gotten along well so far," he'd say. "I'll get along even if I'm weaker."

Consequently, we lived our life with a minimum of anxiety but with more intensity than before. His weakness didn't exclude us from much activity but caused us to do things while we could instead of waiting for some future day. We took long trips, including a Caribbean mission tour and bought a camper for weekend fun. We involved ourselves in church, community, and social activities and had just built a new home on a peaceful, wooded lot.

But as I recalled the past several months, I faced a mounting fear that things were going wrong! Rog's heavy breathing, his continual, quiet coughing, and his total lack of energy scared me. We had just returned from a weekend of camping with friends, and Rog had been so exhausted that he had done almost nothing. His daily headaches were getting more severe. I had seen him drop things and had watched him fall several times recently. For the first time I met depression from a husband who had always radiated optimism. For the first time I saw him troubled and unable to concentrate. I felt I was helplessly standing by watching a disease ruthlessly creep over Rog. What if deterioration would suddenly move fast?

Something was drastically wrong, and the echoing sounds of the swimmers stung my ears. I hurried Chad and Dereck out of the water. We had to return to our room and be near Daddy who was taking a nap. I needed the security of his presence to ward off these hounding fears.

# IT CAN'T BE
# HAPPENING TO ME!

The motel key turned. I wanted to talk but
saw that Rog was still sleeping. For an hour
or so I tried to keep Chad and Dereck quiet.
It was unlike Rog to sleep as much as he had
the past three days since our arrival at the
clinic, but he needed this nap because his night
had been so restless. He could hardly make it
out of bed for breakfast.

Suddenly Rog sat up and called me to the
bed. He grabbed tightly onto my arm. The
startled look on his face and his mumbled

21

words about doing something great frightened me. I thought he was having a hallucination and told him I was going for the doctor. I ran to the clinic. Tearfully, I explained Rog's complete exhaustion and strange talk. The doctor said he would come to the room shortly.

When I returned, Rog was sleeping so peacefully that I felt embarrassed about my hysterical interruption. I rocked Dereck to sleep, then propped my legs on the bed and played several games with Chad, quietly so Rog could sleep.

Suddenly, I looked at Rog and noticed that his lips were closed. He had been breathing deeply through his mouth. I thought, "Good, he's really resting now." Then, like a cloud of heavy air suffocating me, I sensed that Rog wasn't breathing. Frantically, I shook him and I called his name. I felt the center of my being convulse with the knowledge that he was gone.

Somehow, I called the ambulance. A neighbor lady, who was sitting outside our door watching the swimmers, went for the doctor and asked her daughters to take the boys. I endured the twenty-mile drive to the hospital with complete numbness. I knew Rog was gone and the trip was hopeless. It was just a formality — a trip to pronounce my husband dead.

The emergency room was a far cry from the dramatic hospital versions on television. Answering over and over the same questions posed by the doctor, the coroner, and the investigators and filling out forms in routine fashion added to the unreal feeling that was beginning to surround me.

This couldn't be happening to me! My mind ran wild with jumbled thoughts. Death couldn't just sneak in right before my eyes! I'd always felt safe as long as I had my little family together. Death wasn't supposed to happen like this! He's only twenty-nine. He can't just stop breathing. Why didn't I realize something was wrong when he acted so listless? He wasn't supposed to die. The specialist said the progress of the disease would be slow. Victims of muscular dystrophy never die while they are still walking.

It couldn't have happened, but it did. I was signing an autopsy release. I was calling back to Ohio. I was making arrangements for the company plane to come for us. I was being escorted back to the motel room — alone.

# HOW DO YOU SAY,
## "DADDY IS DEAD"?

As I entered the motel, Chad spotted me and came running. "Please God, he is so innocent and happy," I thought. He tugged on my arm and eagerly asked the words I dreaded, "Is Daddy going to be all right?"

How do you tell a six-year-old boy that the Daddy he loves so much is dead? As I looked into his questioning eyes, I knew that the way I handled Rog's death with Chad would set the tone for the whole crisis.

Oh, I had told Chad about death many times.

When he'd stun me with his inquisitiveness about death, I'd intellectually repeat the right words about our bodies dying and us moving on to be with God. But I had never emotionally internalized my belief. Although I wanted to pass on confidence to our children, I was really uncomfortable with thoughts of death.

I had been almost totally untouched by death for twenty-nine years. Except for the death of a friend's child, I had not been close to a crisis of any kind. To say life had been good to me is an understatement. I was a tagalong child with two older brothers, three older sisters, and caring parents who gave me abundant love and attention. Friendship, achievement, and the good life had come with little difficulty. Except for Rog's illness, my life had gone exactly as I wanted it.

Whenever we discussed death with friends, or whenever Rog and I stayed awake and let one of our late-hour talks turn to death, I became restless. I liked my life here so much, I couldn't conceive of an unknown better life to come. My laughing remark to Rog wishing God would send someone back to reassure us about what lies beyond death was really quite serious. Some nights I'd lay awake with an empty feeling gnawing in my stomach as I imagined the grave and not being here.

Belief has never come easy for me. I remember as a ten-year-old child standing on the church steps wondering, "What if this story of Christ is all made up?" My questioning mind welcomed the education of the early sixties when it was in vogue to sit around intellectualizing all kinds of philosophies. Whether an idea was "reasonable" seemed the ultimate test of any belief.

A friend asked me once, "Janette, are you sure you can take the path of doubting and return to faith?" I never really stopped believing. In fact, the years of our marriage brought a great deal of spiritual growth for me. Yet I did face recurring questions about God, the mystical salvation event, and immortality.

Now as I faced this horribly personal experience with death, I felt assured beyond all doubt that dying literally involves moving to a higher plain of existence. The presence of God was so real!

How grateful I was that Chad's previous questioning had forced me to explain death to him so that he was familiar with the concept of the inner self as something separate from the outer body. Calmly and with complete confidence, I told Chad, "Daddy's body was too sick to live. The part of him we loved is with God now." He understood as well as his young mind could comprehend.

The secure peace that surrounded me was unbelievable. The painful days and months ahead would bring emotions so crushing that the religious experience which now cradled me would be needed badly.

# THE COMFORT OF
# FAMILY AND FRIENDS

Until the plane arrived to take us back to
Ohio, my sons and I had four hours alone. We
cried, we clung to each other, and we talked
about our good life with Daddy. We had time
to try placing the reality that he was gone in
our uncomprehending minds.

Chad showed great affection and wanted to
pack all of Rog's things himself. Dereck fluctuated between scenes of tears and periods of
play. As I look back, I'm sure the boys' adjustment was made easier because they were told

the facts, were allowed to share in my grief, and were immediately assured that although Daddy was gone, I was still there to love and care for them.

To keep children out of a home where death has occurred, to shield them from reality because "we don't want to upset them" seems wrong to me. I feel strongly that sometime soon after death occurs, the children involved need to be told the facts, including the general cause of the death. Otherwise, they may fantasize that the parent died because they were naughty or that the parent abandoned them.

Dereck, especially, viewed Rog as omnipotent. He needed to be assured that his father did not *choose* to leave him. Unless told the physical reason — illness or accident — a child may be afraid that he or the remaining parent may die soon too. Chad and Dereck would face enough uncertainty in the next several months without letting them imagine things that could be explained now.

Not only did we need that time alone in the motel as a family, huddling together to ward off the terrible change that Rog's death meant, but we needed other people. How we needed others! I needed to be held in loving arms. I needed the comfort of crying on the shoulders of people who would hold me close.

Four dear friends and my sister, who had received my call and had the awful task of telling the news to others, came on the private plane. I was anxious for them to arrive, yet meeting them was unbearably sad. I wanted to fall into their arms, hoping to be shielded from the harsh reality that I just had gone through. The comfort of their embraces was a staying force for me. Our parents and some of the brothers and sisters waited till early morning for our plane to touch down in Ohio. They held me and cried with me too. Just being together in our pain assured me that I would not be alone.

I needed to know that other hearts ached too. Mary Ann, one of the friends who came on the plane, stayed with me all through that long night. Her husband and the two other friends drove our car back from Wisconsin. She said few words of comfort but cried and shared the pain of grief.

The next three days the word "support" took on a new, warm meaning for me which seemed to say that in the face of death not much else matters. A constant flow of friends and relatives expressed their love. Virg and Mary Ann and Dick and Lou Ann were around much of that first day. Knowing that their lives had stopped too was a great comfort to me. The presence of Carolyn and Mary Ann, organizing the house and food, meant much and gave me some sense of security.

The simple acts of bringing a dish of food, taking the boys for an afternoon of play, cleaning the house, serving meals, and helping select music for the memorial service told me of the concern of a wide circle of other friends. Never again will I minimize the value of people physically "working out" grief.

The warm personal notes which mentioned Rog and assured me of their prayers gave me emotional support. The many gifts — the beautiful flowers, plants, and memorial gifts — which before seemed a useless tradition, now took on deep meaning as I thought of the relationship that each of the senders had with Rog.

The two days prior to the funeral were a blur of decisions: making the arrangements ("The burial must be first; I refuse to follow the casket out of the church"); picking the casket ("Does it really matter which vault is more waterproof?"); planning the service ("Choose something from his life to encourage others, not just a sermon"); the obituary ("I'll write, I can't stand impersonal statistics"); and the funeral visitation ("None of that limp handshaking; let's make it a sharing time").

In the past, visiting the funeral home had always been a dreadful occasion for me. I would think of any possible excuse to avoid going. When all failed and I had to go, I approached the bereaved family thinking I must say the "right words" of comfort and somehow console them in their loss. Standing in line, with my hands turning cold and lumps forming in my throat, I would disconcertingly find that I could think of nothing to say. It certainly wouldn't be good to talk about the deceased, especially if the family seemed to be "taking it so well." My tears and comments would just reopen wounds and cause them to lose control, I thought. So I usually resorted to some nice little phrase and tried to hide my emotions because after all I had come to comfort them.

As I stood by Rog's body, I found I wanted to talk about him. Hearing about the significance of his life seemed to make his death less tragic. I wanted to cling to people who shared something about him or talked of activity we had done together, because here was part of Rog's life walking before me! Talking about the quality of his life somehow made the fact that it had been cut so short seem less futile.

Recalling his life made the separation less harsh. Being told that a void was left in the business, that his leadership at church and in several organizations would be missed, and that his friendship would be hard to replace affirmed the great loss that I was feeling.

I didn't care to recite over and over the detail's of Rog's death and at times felt that some people seemed more concerned with how I was taking it than with sadness that he was gone. A great part of giving sympathy is simply listening and reacting to the feelings expressed by the bereaved. A sensitive ear will hear what the family wants to talk about.

Those who came and cried and shared a feeling of loss were much more supporting than those who came as "comforters" and said nice words. Canned phrases about "life must go on" and Bible quotes about "the mysteries of God" and "the goodness of God's will," especially when quoted by those who had not faced a devasting death, seemed glib indeed!

# ADMITTING FRIGHTENING EMOTIONS

I returned from the memorial service dazed but composed. The huge church had been full, an indication of the many good people who supported us. Love and care had been given generously. I felt blessed by the warm sharing of the community and was gratified by the many concerned prayers. My faith in God and immortality gave good reason for courage. I felt a strength that was more than my own!

However, keeping a brave front and being center stage had also forced me to have stamina. I function well under pressure. Being in front of an audience has always brought the best out of me. I was aware that I wanted to act strong, as a compliment and final tribute to Rog. Over and over people said, "If anyone can take this and raise two boys alone, Janette can."

The first several weeks after the funeral are vague and almost nonexistent in my memory. I know I was kept busy with thank-you notes, reading mail, and receiving phone calls and visitors as well as sadly throwing out wilted bouquets and making necessary financial decisions. I realize that I dropped one by one the strong-faced defenses that I had worn during the funeral and drifted into an unreal, dazed state. I remember that I allowed myself to be taken care of. My appetite was completely gone and when I wasn't serving the boys leftovers, I guess someone was around to cook. My mother must have done the washing and some of the cleaning during her frequent visits those first weeks. The boys were kept occupied, often by friends and relatives.

I recall that I took the phone off the hook and napped all afternoon. My perfect dreams of Rog gave relief to the cruel reality I faced. I needed sleep so that I could stay up late, talking to whichever friend or relative came to spend the night. To release the guilt I felt because I hadn't realized Rog was so sick, I had to talk about his illness. I had to talk about my love for him and recall the past — the beautiful past.

Those early weeks were spelled RETREAT —
a retreat from a life always scheduled with
interesting plans, into a kind of seclusion from
society. I just wanted to stay in our home,
which we had worked on so hard, which we
had moved into only four months earlier. This
was my world. Here I could shake off the unfamiliar insecurity that was beginning to en-
circle me.

Three weeks after Rog died, I struggled to
get out from under the daze. I made a valiant
effort to lift my face. I was tired of depending
on others to do things for me. The strain of
having someone around each night so I wouldn't
need to be alone began to wear on me. I was
29 years old. It was time to pull things together and take care of myself. Fortunately, I
found a young schoolteacher who was interested
in renting our guest room. When Joyce moved
in, I told her that I was tired of company and
would treat her as a member of the household.
She was relieved as much as I, and the situation worked out well.

I decided it was time to do as everyone kept
telling me and "get out." I tried hard. Hiding
my horrible insecurity behind a smile, I pleas-
antly answered "fine" when asked how I was
doing.

But everything seemed so grotesquely unreal! Shopping made me physically sick. Tears
filled my eyes whenever I'd push the cart
past all those people who were smugly going
about their daily living while my whole world
had fallen apart.

Going away was such an effort. I couldn't even make the simple decision of what to wear! Attending church was harrowing — the empty seat was traumatic.

Mopping floors at home was probably the most upsetting of all. The futility of doing "wifely functions" when I wasn't a wife anymore left me completely undone.

As weeks passed, I became more and more aware of frightening emotions and feelings churning within me. Attempts to smother and ignore them did little good. All the nice clichés that "life is for the living" were no help at all. I knew I needed to shape up and go on, but how? My loss became so overwhelming that being told awful tales about people who had experienced things much worse than I brought no relief. I was already sadly aware that there were millions of starving people and that much of the world's population faced war and death every day. Yes, I had lost *only* my husband and still had the children.

I tried to agree with those who said that death is easier than divorce. I looked around me and agreed that I had everything I wanted, except Rog. Yet the pain was still so great that the comparative suffering of others brought no healing.

My friends tried to help by keeping me busy. The first several months I had invitations to all kinds of places: "I have an extra ticket and thought you might enjoy. . . ." "Let's go to. . . ." "Wouldn't it be fun to. . . ." Knowing that opportunities were there helped. At least

I didn't feel abandoned in my grief. Although I did accept many offers, most activity had lost its meaning and its fun.

I became so lonesome for Rog. Missing him made my whole body feel weak. I experienced a real physical emptiness that never left me. The knot in my chest found release only in hard sobbing. At times my eyes looked vacant and hollow and often I couldn't concentrate. The heavy sigh that came from deep within me was an indication of the growing grief that was settling over me.

Rog died August 23. September 6 would have been his thirtieth birthday. Several days later I sent Chad off to school — a fatherless child. On September 26 I halfheartedly tried to celebrate Dereck's fourth birthday and on October 23 I tried to keep Chad busy with a small after-school party. By Thanksgiving I was in deep despair, thinking that I just couldn't endure anymore alone.

I seemed to be sinking under uncontrollable emotions. Before Rog died I had read about the stages of grief. Intellectually I had agreed that denial, anger, guilt, and depression are natural.

After his death, I read more books about the normal process of grief. Sometimes I was unbelievably analytical and coldly observed myself reacting in certain ways. Yet knowing what was going on inside me didn't take away the frustration and the guilt that I wasn't strong enough to control my emotions.

# FACING
# RAW GRIEF

How was I to cope with Rog's death and what grief was doing to me? My hopes and dreams lay smashed to bits. I wasn't certain that I could salvage anything from the pieces — or if I even wanted to. Continually reminding myself that I was a strong, religious, sane person didn't always make me act strongly, trustingly, or sanely.

During the third to sixth months, especially, my emotional reactions were so raw and unpredictable that I had little control over them.

Some days an agonizing emptiness gnawed within me. I didn't know how to handle the totally foreign emotion of wanting to give up and die. At other times I faced deep depression and no feeling at all. Sometimes I'd experience a negative bitterness that suffocated my spirit. Then, surprisingly, intermingled between these bad days would come peaceful interludes when I felt that I would be able to handle Rog's death after all.

These reactions didn't come in any observable pattern but were cyclical and jumbled. I thought coping with death would be like climbing a mountain. Once I had gone through the progressive stages, I would come out on top with the victory flag of ACCEPTANCE in my hand. I wasn't prepared for grief's slow walk over a dusty road where each bend seemed to bring again a path that I thought I had already traveled.

What does a person do when emotions are so clouded that life loses its attraction and purpose? During those months I sometimes found myself asking, "Why continue here?" The popular song with the words, "I won't live a day without you" plaintively echoed my feelings. At times I felt that my whole reason for living had been swallowed up by Rog's death. I had been comfortable in my role as Rog's wife and had found much of my identity in relation to him. I just didn't know how I could live without Rog. I had depended on our marriage for so much of my happiness.

Oh, I was sure that I would never physically take my life, but at times I lived with near suicidal wishes when death with its absence of problems seemed appealing. Why couldn't I just join Rog and have it all over? I entertained the idea that the boys might be better off raised by a couple who could give them a fun, happy life like ours was supposed to have been. I was just painfully existing; functioning but in a living death. The color had gone out of my life.

These feelings absolutely horrified me! Life and its activities had always been exciting. Many times I had sat in Sunday school class agreeing that Christians should be people of joy. Long faces hindered our witness of hope. Christians should be people with purpose, of all persons most blessed! Consequently, when I saw myself considering life an effort and certainly not much of a blessing, I felt terribly ugly inside and extremely guilty too.

This sort of "chin up, Christians don't struggle" view of life did little more than help me put on a smiling face to hide a torn heart. I knew a surface job wouldn't work for me. I needed to search, to meditate, and to work through my mind this hard grief if I were ever again unequivocally to say yes to life. Often I pleaded, "God, I don't want to spend the rest of my life withering away. Help me work it out! Help me see life as good."

Observing other widows who have remained on this path of "just existing" scared me. Joyless people turn others away. I knew I needed people. The excitement I heard in the voices of the boys as they related something that interested them warned me that I dare not chip away their lives with my defeat. Knowing the boys needed me helped clear my clouded emotions and gave me the reason I needed to go on living.

The human mind can be fragile. Who can say where the breaking point lies? It was frightening to feel the horrible emotions which can lead to a mental breakdown. At times I faced deep and exhausting depression, when my weariness physically immobolized me and I didn't want to function or feel at all. Not having the energy to care if anything got done, I slept a lot to escape. Withdrawing under the warm covers and turning my mind off provided relief from a reality that was too painful to face. I went through times of near oblivion when I didn't know or care what was happening outside myself and the boys. I was uninterested in national and community events or news items which had always seemed important before.

During those days of draining depression I thought that I'd never have the stamina to endure grief and that falling apart would be so much easier than coping. I wanted to shock people's you're-doing-so-well theory and shout, "I need your help. You're ignoring my pain."

When I was low I had neither the energy nor the boldness to shout, but I knew that without help I couldn't handle this depression which was so out of character for me. Thank God I had friends who sensed when I needed to talk, accepted my bad times as natural, and cried when I cried. Those friends who stuck by me, even though I had no energy to give to the relationship, seemed to know when I needed a late evening phone call or a long conversation of encouragement. Without those listeners, the retreat into depression may have defeated me.

Disappointment can destroy a person. Becoming buried in self-pity was another of my reactions to Rog's death. At times I spent futile effort wondering why — why the death? Or why the disease in the first place? Why did Rog who embodied the words, "I have so much to live for," have to allow a disease to waste him away? Why weren't we granted the miracle of healing? Why with modern medicine can't there be a hint of a cure for muscular dystrophy? Why must we sit and watch it unrelentingly destroy a body? Bitterness at a society which spends billions for bombs but a pittance for research crept into my being.

Pessimism settled in slyly and unnoticed, until one day I realized what a negative person I was becoming. I saw myself emphasizing problems, heard my voice losing its enthusiasm, and faced the fact that everything seemed so bad there was nothing good to talk about.

How utterly frightening it is to watch yourself becoming cynical. "Life is just a series of deaths," I heard myself saying. "Your bubble will burst too, everything ends." "You call that a problem?" Before, I had been bored by people with completely negative natures and ingeniously avoided them. Now I felt too nearly like them for comfort! When I realized I was sitting on my chair with my broken dreams, becoming bitter and old, I knew I had to get hold of myself. I was on the wrong road!

I had to work hard not to become jealous of what others still had. Making a conscious effort not to let envy get in the way of friendships took time. Recognizing my bitterness about my turn of fate, holding it out where I could see and understand it, made it less powerful over me. We must admit bitterness before we are able to reject it. Smothering the feeling will not work. I desperately wanted the boys to catch Rog's optimism and not my negativeness.

Between these awful times, I had many days which were surprisingly good — days when I consciously refused to let grief conquer me and clung to a sense of hope that I would make it. For periods of time I could release my feelings to God and bravely say, "If Rog is with You, I can make the best of what is left." I had days when a natural kind of self-preservation flowed through my veins and I felt confident that eventually stability would return. There were days when Rog's last conversation on death, which left me with the words, "I know you would go on if anything happened to me," burned strength into my heart.

Ours was not a house of death. There was no morbid atmosphere hanging in the rooms. I tried to empty my emotions in private so

42

the boys wouldn't be afraid. Laughter often caught us unaware. Suddenly, in surprise, I'd realize that we were having a good time. My coping days were unbelievably peaceful and sometimes lasted for weeks. During such periods I felt that Rog would be smiling, because I knew he'd expect me to give the boys as much joy as possible in spite of his death.

The cyclical, fluctuating nature of grief was extremely hard for me. I felt so defeated when my good state would slip away and I was unable to bring it back. I felt not only anger at myself but also at Rog, because I thought that if the situation were reversed, he'd be coping so much better. Then I wanted to shake my fist at his optimism and his "make the best of everything" attitude. Praise given to me during my good days, "You're doing so much better," vibrated hollowly through my mind when I'd fall again into one of the other three moods. I was discouraged that I seemed so powerless to control my reactions.

After months of being disheartened by my instability, I gradually realized that healing would come through accepting my emotions and admitting that it was futile to try to avoid the natural feelings of painful grief. Only by understanding my reactions could I ever hope to pull away from their power to control me. Being so hard on myself only added guilt to the strain. I needed to learn compassion for myself instead of self-criticism and comparison with Rog. The walk was mine, not his, and I would have to cope in my own way. I had to stop berating myself with, "How can I have such terrible emotions?" and ask instead, "What do I do with such feelings?"

I saw that it was going to be a continuous struggle to make my days of acceptance and feeling good outnumber my days of emptiness, depression, and fear. Great comfort came with the knowledge that God was quietly standing by, understanding my walk through the valley. I felt great relief when I realized that I didn't have to prove how strong I was.

# LETTING
# GO SLOWLY

Going on without Rog was first of all an inner struggle. The emotional heartbreak and problems of coping had to be worked out by me. No one could walk the long, dusty road of grief for me. Yet, the people who surrounded me those first six months had much to do with the recovery process.

Most people feel more and more awkward as they continue to relate to someone in grief. After the funeral, what should they do? Touching, for most people, stays in the funeral parlor. Not knowing what to say or do, many replace the comforting words and feelings of closeness with meaningless chatter. I knew others were thinking about my loss and they knew I was thinking about it. But instead of saying how we felt, we handled the whole matter delicately and avoided talking about it.

Meekly I suffered through all those looks of pity, agreed that the weather was nice, and endured the pain as everyone gently rubbed the boys' heads and said, "My, aren't those (fatherless) boys sweet?"

What do you say to someone who recently has buried a loved one? For most of us it seems easier to avoid the whole thing than to take the chance of bringing on tears. I remember years ago standing in the kitchen of friends who had buried their young son six months earlier. We were having a family picnic. When I saw the boy's picture hanging on the wall, I started to say, "I know you really miss him when you see all our children playing together. I wish he could be here!" The words never came out, because I was afraid we'd all cry.

Now I say, "What's wrong with a few tears?" It was good to have some people say, "We're glad you came even though it is hard! We're praying you will be able to go on without him." Crying is better than ignoring.

The first several months I wanted to talk about Rog — about missing him, about the importance of life and death, and about the past. I had loved Rog. My whole being had been tied to his. His life was so important to me; it couldn't suddenly be gone. To have his absence go unmentioned by well-meaning people left me miserable and lonely. I wanted to shout, "Doesn't anyone miss him but me?"

Few people seemed to have any concept of what giving up Rog was doing to me. I needed acknowledgement that letting go of someone I loved *was* intensely painful. Releasing Rog to an existence I could neither understand nor experience could only come by confirming the value his life had been. I needed talk and understanding, not the silent pity which at times seemed so heavy that I could physically feel it pressing down upon me.

Must Sunday school classes go on with their nice little routine discussions when my heart is breaking? Must family gatherings and social functions obviously attempt to ignore my deep feelings? At Thanksgiving no one mentioned Rog's name except one innocent little nephew who said, "Oh, your daddy isn't here is he?"

Fortunately, I had a group of friends who nursed me through this period of wanting to talk about Rog and about death. Although I'm sure they found it difficult, they understood that the future was too painful to face yet and the only way to look was back! These people interspersed their conversation with "Rog would have said. . ." and "Remember when Rog. . .?" They could honestly say, "I miss him so much today" or "He could have helped me with this." By Christmas some of my relatives realized that I needed to hear Rog's name included in our celebration.

Perhaps some people can best cope with death by never again mentioning the name of the dead person. We all have different degrees of needing to recall. A recently bereaved father told me that he now understood another father who before had annoyed him with frequent references to his dead son. "If we had listened to him and understood his need, he wouldn't still be recalling the past so much."

Years ago, a widow was expected to mourn and pay homage to her husband for a year. She could be openly sad and was expected to talk about her dead husband with love and respect. Although I certainly would hate to dress in black and be socially restricted for a year, perhaps the old forms of mourning more clearly recognized the grief process than our modern society. Today too many people not only try to deny death, but also expect the dead to be put away as quickly and with as little pain as possible. Almost as soon as the last bouquet has wilted, we're told, "You're just going to have to get over this!"

Grief is multiplied and recovery is much slower and more lonely when people refuse to allow us to look back. They feel awkward discussing memories of the dead and may fear "she may live in the past too long."

My grief experience has taught me that detaching ourselves emotionally from the dead comes neither smoothly nor quickly. But it will be better accomplished by honest recall than by smothering such thoughts and forcing us to face the future before we've come to terms with the lost past.

48

# INTENSE ABOUT
# IMMORTALITY

During the first six months I needed to talk about Rog so that I could gradually let go. But I also became overwhelmingly interested in immortality. Suddenly it was such a personal subject; my husband was there. All kinds of questions hounded me.

Had Rog known he was dying when he called me to his bed with that strange look and those words of surprise? Why didn't I listen to him longer? The unquestioning peace that Rog was with God which I felt so strongly those first few days — was that real or just my feeling?

I read all kinds of books, and prayer became more meaningful. Some days I would be on such a high spiritual plane that I was almost detached from this world.

Other days the terrible emotional problems brought on by coping with life without Rog and my natural tendency to reason things out threw me into a feeling of total separation from God. How could I think there was a God who could care personally about my problem? Maybe He didn't really exist after all and the idea of immortality was just man's way of coping with the harsh reality of death. Sometimes it seemed the more I asked God to reveal Himself to me, the more silent He was!

Eventually, the belief that "God is there" settled firmly and quietly in my heart, but questions about immortality buffeted me with full force. Unlike those dear people who can so simply say, "God will take care of it," and go happily on their way, I became intensely interested in what immortality meant for Rog. It was as if I needed to know that being with God was something Rog would be vitally enjoying right now. Then I could pull myself from under the fog and enjoy life here again.

I read everything about heaven and the afterlife that I could find — from the most traditional to the most unfamiliar. A few talked about oblivion until the resurrection, because God's time is unlike our time and a thousand years is as a day with Him. Some told me Rog was in a material place (probably taking care of God's books since he was a businessman) except that sin was removed. Others believed that in a mystical sort of way our spirits are again united with the God-force after death and that is our resurrection.

A few talked about the exciting possibility of growth toward complete knowledge of God. After death we simply continue growing from where we are here. Many mansions means many levels of personal awareness and growth. God-knowledge has little to do with age or mental capacity but with how well we have learned God's unselfish love. Others disagreed. If you're "under the blood," you're all the same. Death automatically makes you all-knowing and heaven is everyone praising God with one voice.

Some told me that I should believe what I wanted. "We make our own heaven. Whatever we think, that's what it will be for us," they said. Others were dogmatically sure that heaven and the resurrection are spelled out explicitly in the Bible. The signs are so clear that Christ will return soon, so why worry about time?

Periodically my search became grimly serious. I wanted to know the *truth*, not just what made me feel good or helped me cope. My search became frustratingly mixed up. Which interpretation of the Bible could I believe? I seriously prayed for a vision of Rog living in peace. Other people had them. "Please God, why can't I?"

My search was also at rare moments light and humorous. I could imagine myself search-

ing through all those millions of souls to find
Rog. I wished immortality would be an issue
to vote on. If ninety percent of the church
felt a certain way, it would be like that. My
friends and I laughed at more heaven jokes
than ever before.

Most of all my search was intensely stimulating. From reading and sharing with others,
my mind was expanded by glimpses of possibilities and snatches here and there of poten-
tial hope.

To imagine a life of freedom and fulfillment
where the power of evil is gone and our spiritual wisdom and goodness can grow unhin-
dered is liberating. My mind is enlarged when I
think of the possibility of a time when we'll
have dropped our defenses and our fronts and
recognize the elemental true self in each other
— a time of no competition and comparing.

To envision a situation of meaningful fellowship — a continuation of the *best* we have experienced on earth (or even better) — broadens
my perspective. To contemplate love in a completely new dimension, to imagine that we will
grow till God is the real center of our existence,
and to grasp that man *is* soul not man *has a*
soul — all this leaves my mind beautifully free.
Man-Soul-Personality survives the death of
the body and passes from our inner wheel of
time to God's outer wheel of eternity.

I stand in wonder if I can believe John's vision in the Book of Revelation which he
glimpsed something so utterly indescribable
that he compared it to the most magnificent

things he could think of. I am satisfied if I can give reliability to Paul's words in 2 Corinthians 5:8, "We are of good courage, and we would rather be away from the body and at home with the Lord," and if I give credence to a host of other people who have reported a "leaving of the body" during near-death experiences.

If I accept as authentic the experience of a dear friend, Pauline Holsopple, whose tragic auto accident brought her so near death that she was medically hopeless, I am at peace. She tells of finding herself approaching one of the most beautiful, peaceful experiences imaginable and not wanting to return. Her words, "I get so excited when a Christian dies, because I know what they're experiencing," have fused into my being. She is not a fanatic; perhaps here is my vision.

I have come to accept the saying, "God will take care of it," but it has become personally mine — a meaning I can live with.

9

# DEATH IS BEAUTIFUL?
# I PROTEST!

Although my spiritual side agreed that death is a glorious, even beautiful thing for the dying Christian, my emotions screamed out in protest. Those people who say burying a loved one is no problem if we have faith are unrealistic. "Wait until you face the void and the separation," I plead. "Live through the pain of letting go of a loved one and then try to say it is no problem."

Being cut off from the one person who meant the most to me brought sickening anguish! I still feel the churning reaction whenever I think about the finality of our earthly separation.

I cried tears of indescribable loneliness for several days after I happened upon a box of our old letters in the attic. The three years of letters all neatly in order brought into stark reality all that I had lost! In our dating and in our marriage, I never questioned that Rog loved me. Even in our disagreements I knew I had his acceptance. He was the one person who knew me so well that I had to be honest.

How could I stand never again being surprised by his special gifts and his playful packages and ideas — the dress in the bicycle box or the invitation to dinner pasted on the steering wheel of the car? To know that I'd never again see Rog working at the desk in the study, watch him read a favorite book, or hear him discuss his opinions on an issue made my heart ache. I felt an empty, sick sensation when I admitted that he'd never again come through the kitchen door, never again give me his almost-daily call from the office, or hold his boys on his ready lap.

To bury from my life his quiet, unassuming love and be disconnected forever from his knowing grin, his gentle arms, and the warmth of his physical body was nauseatingly unbeautiful. Closing the lid to an earthly relationship with a husband, a lover, the father of our children, and one of my best friends brought harsh tears of protest!

One cold February day, six months after Rog died, I wrote these words of protest to those

who minimized my loss by beautiful talk about
death.

## THIS THING OF BEAUTY

Death is beautiful,
   I've been told.
At times I wistfully
   agree.

To be with God,
   Eternal joy,
     A higher plain.
Rog has these now in a world
   of greater peace.
Because I don't understand
   and can't experience,
Should I begrudge
   his going?

Death is beautiful,
   I am satisfied.
Till the hollow feeling inside
   reeks with awareness
That I will never again
   in all eternity

Be held as his lover,
   Share his dreams,
     Savor our fun.

My alone and heavy soul
   desperately asks,
What can all this pain
   have to do with beauty?

Yes, I had to protest! How could I ever view Rog's death as a good thing. To expect me quietly to consent to the end of our marriage which had brought so much happiness was unrealistic. I just couldn't approve of death!

Separation from Rog flung me into an unbelievable identity struggle. Before Rog died, I viewed myself as an independent, usually confident person who enjoyed marriage but certainly was not at all the clinging-vine type. If Rog had been asked how much my self-worth concept depended on him, he would have smiled and said, "Little." I kept telling myself that life had been good before I knew Rog. I got along fine then; I would just have to do it again.

Yet seven months after he died, I was still fighting an awful insecurity. How much I had depended on Rog's love and acceptance backing me so that I could be aggressive, free, and confident became unsettlingly clear. I had stood in his reflection for more of my identity than I had realized. I had spent nine years fitting my life into his, getting used to certain patterns of living, and relying on his support. Now I felt that half of me was dead and I absolutely didn't know how to cope with being disjointed!

When I read books by widows who found their husband's death not only an awful crisis, but also a kind of liberation into independence, new careers, and more education, I sighed. I already had as much freedom and education as I wanted. Instead of Rog's death making me more self-reliant, I seemed to be changing into a weak, dependent person. Grief was horribly affecting my personality, and I didn't know what to do about it except get angry at myself for feeling so helpless inside. Instead of drawing on my own strength, I reverted to a childlike wish that Rog would be here to take care of me. Yet that was not a realistic recollection of our relationship.

If I were honest, I knew I could learn to take care of things, although that loomed large. In our marriage we had shared most responsibilities but I had paid little attention to those areas where Rog was definitely more competent. Consequently, I had never balanced the checkbook or considered finances and knew little about the maintenance of the house or yard. After I had overcome the shock, I also knew I would be decisive in important matters. What I didn't possess, at this point, was the strength to see that our life could have much meaning or happiness without Rog.

I could be on the road to accepting his death as something that could not be changed. I could decide to handle depression and bitterness. I could grasp the hope of immortality and determine that we should go on. But as long as I felt like a half-a-person, one ripped apart and disjointed, there could be only intermittent relief from the heaviness that settled on my soul.

# HELPING
# CHILDREN COPE

What was happening to our two small boys during all those months of personal struggle with Rog's death? During the first months, I did a lot of sighing and muttering to myself. "There's no way I can raise two boys alone."

We have been a very close family; it was easy to understand that Chad and Dereck would feel deeply hurt and insecure. But I had no one to counsel me, no authority on how to help children cope with the death of a parent.

At times I was so overwhelmed by my own sorrow that I ignored their hurt. When I was under, I'm sure they felt that I considered them a big part of the burden that life had become. Often I neglected to tell them how much I loved them and how much I needed their love in return.

Fortunately, along with the mistakes of those early months there were fragments of things that helped the boys adjust. From the first I felt the boys needed to be given something to hang on to. By emphasizing what they still had, I hoped to keep them from sinking under the despair that battered me. Telling Chad and Dereck about all the remaining good things in our life forced me to verbalize them to myself.

Sometimes our prayers of thanks at bedtime seemed hollow and gratitude wasn't always evident in our voices, but we continued. Over and over we reiterated the fact that God loves us, that He takes care of us, and He is taking care of Daddy. We thanked God for the many people who care for us, for our good community, and for the fact that we still had each other.

The reality that Rog was no longer present as a model for the boys was unbearably sad to me. I shared his value system and his view of life and wanted the boys to catch some of his traits. For a child suddenly to be cut off from the caring that a parent gives is devastating. I wanted the boys to know that if he were still alive, Rog would vitally care about what they were doing.

Intermingled in our conversation those first

months were comments like, "Dereck, Daddy would be happy today because you cooperated so well. He felt doing a good job was important." Or, "Chad, your father would be proud if he could see how you can hit the ball and how well you're doing in school."

I had to check myself so that I didn't overdo such comments or use them in a threatening sort of way, as if Daddy were watching so they'd better not be naughty. There were periods of time, especially at bedtime, when Chad covered his ears and didn't want to hear Rog's name mentioned because he didn't want to cry. I understood and followed his wishes, but was relieved when later he moved through that painful stage and could again happily recall his father.

To keep from glamorizing Rog to the boys was terribly difficult. Rog had been a good father. Chad and Dereck deserved to remember that they had a father who helped around the house, dropped out of several clubs to spend more time with the family, and viewed bedtime as listening time for his boys.

They heard a lot of praise of him before he died and they must have been smothered by it afterward. One October day when I was disciplining Chad, he glared at me. He wished Dad were here, he sobbed, because Dad never got mad or punished him. I knew that I couldn't compete with a father who had become larger than life in Chad's eyes. All small children think their dad is the biggest, the smartest, and the best, and if he dies he takes on almost supernatural qualities. I tempered my comments about Rog with as much realism as possible after that.

The first several months I was filled with the idea that I didn't want the boys to forget Rog. They were so young. Would they remember him? If I had died, I would want them to recall things about me. Our family picture albums, which are done in diary form for each year of our lives, became very precious to me — a way of linking the boys with their past. The first weekend I went away, I locked them in the safe. The whole large house could burn, as far as I was concerned, as long as my pictures — my most important possession — escaped unharmed.

Good memories are a precious gift, especially to the child who feels alone. Recalling good times, humorous incidents, and tender moments should not become a substitute for living in the present, but they can provide a continuity between past and future for the child who has lost a parent.

My chest tightened everytime I thought of all that death had taken from Chad and Dereck. They had been cheated out of a father's love, his caring concern, and gentle affection. I would not cheat them out of their memories and a sense of relationship with Rog. I had to help them through this time of transition so the separation would not be so abrupt.

# AVOIDING
# DRASTIC CHANGES

In spite of all my efforts to make the cutoff from their father less brutal, Daddy was dead, and Chad and Dereck faced sweeping emotional adjustments.

At first whenever Dereck was sad, angry, or just unhappy, he'd cry for his daddy. All his little problems ended in tears for Rog, which was understandable because as an adult I was doing the same thing, only in a more refined way. Every night at bedtime Dereck sobbed out his loss. "I can't hug and kiss Daddy anymore!

Why can't God send Daddy back?" He was much more expressive about his pain than Chad was, but he could follow his outbursts with fun and laughter.

Chad went through stages of shock. He became sullen and upset when he needed disciplining. "You don't like me," he'd shout. He faced stages of insecurity when he thought he wasn't wanted by me or his friends. Once he blurted out, "You wish I'd die too," when he felt crushed by the bad situation. Mostly he was just quiet about his hurt. And I didn't give him as much help as I could have.

Both Chad and Dereck were keenly aware of the emptiness in our family without a father. Almost immediately they suggested, "We can get another daddy, can't we?" My emotions were so tight that I cried and didn't listen to the need of assured love behind their plea. Consequently, for the first several months we had a recurring conversation. I kept telling them, "You *had* a great daddy. Not just any daddy would be as nice." They kept asking, "When will we find a new daddy?" and accusing, "You don't want a daddy, do you?"

After I learned more about accepting their need as natural and as a beautiful compliment to Rog, I assured them that we were still very much a family, and that I wouldn't discount the idea of a new father. Chad understood and relaxed, because now he could still hope. Dereck solved the problem with, "Well, if I can't have a daddy, could I have a puppy to love?"

Emotional problems were enough to live with those first months. Those young widows who face financial burdens, too, have an almost unmanagable load. Characteristic of Rog's thoroughness, he left us financially solvent. The salary which his company continued for the rest of the year made money worries unnecessary. Then with social security coming in, I knew I could take time to decide whether I wanted a job.

When I was offered a teaching position in January, I felt a bit guilty that I couldn't swing it yet. Grief brings with it an apathetic laziness and lack of energy. Just thinking about the schedule of teaching each day, taking Dereck to the sitter, and grading papers in the evening when I'd rather be spending time with Chad left me exhausted. I didn't feel capable of handling what a change in schedules would do to our already-upset household. Keeping the house in some kind of order and doing the simple routines seemed a giant enough task. Convinced that the boys needed me at home, I silently thanked Rog again and again that he had left us able to avoid any more drastic changes that first year.

Avoiding drastic change — I was warned that this was necessary for the boys' healthy adjustment. Sometimes I wanted to scream, "But our life *has* changed drastically; I can't pretend it hasn't." I wanted to mash the teeth of the cliché, "We must go on living." When people told me, "You can't let this ruin your life," I wanted to hammer away with the words, "It can't be the same, it can't be the same. The life we knew is ruined!" Yet no matter how much I fought the idea, I knew that we had to do some of the same things that had given order and meaning to our lives if we hoped to survive as a family.

Sitting in a pew at church, which should be a most comforting place for a grieving family, was lonely and upsetting. Church was the one place I never went alone; worship and family belonged together. Now I not only had to contend with two restless children by myself, but I had to worry about controlling my emotions as well. For months, music brought tears to my eyes. The songs were so personally meaningful; I had never noticed before how many mention heaven and departed loved ones.

Celebrating special days or watching the boys accomplish something new brought on a siege of insufferable loneliness. "If only Rog could see them today," echoed in my ears all day and I realized how much he was missing here. I wept to God, "Immortality had better be good if he has to miss watching his boys mature!"

After hitting that bottom slump over Thanksgiving, when I thought I just couldn't endure anymore celebrations alone, I was determined to make Christmas happy for the boys. The calendar schedule became full and I was glad. Many people dropped in and we had several families over for meals so our house was lively. Trimming the tree brought sentimental lumps in our throats, especially when we pulled out the big star that Rog had helped Chad make several years before. My parents came over on Christmas Eve when we opened our presents. It wasn't like having Daddy here, but it helped!

As each month went by, I saw that there were more and more things that I could handle by myself. There wasn't much choice.

# BEING AN
# ONLY PARENT

How was I going to raise Chad and Dereck alone? What would happen to discipline and the whole atmosphere of our home without a father? Of the opinion that many problems in contemporary family life relate to the absentee father figure, I was very threatened by the outcome of raising Chad and Dereck alone.

The thought of being totally responsible for two boys overwhelmed me. I worried whether I was too tough or too lenient, and whether I was demanding too much responsibility or not enough. Rog and I acted as a balance and support for each other, keeping ourselves levelheaded about problems and discipline.

By winter I panicked with the possibility that it would be all my fault if they turned out wrong. I fussed about their personalities. Their natural naughty stages were suddenly not as acceptable to me. The picking on each other — the little kick, the teasing laugh, or the slight shove which ends in a tussle with someone usually getting hurt — nearly drove me up the wall. I couldn't remember that they had acted like that when Rog was here. I certainly must be raising them wrong. They're growing into hurtful and unfeeling people, I thought. I found myself yelling in anger much too often, "Why can't you get along? You're supposed to love each other."

Before when I had bad times with the boys, Rog was there to relieve me. When we went away or had guests, he was there helping the boys dress and keeping things moving smoothly. Now there was just me. I knew I had to handle each situation by myself. I dreaded the process of getting ready to go away and often stayed home because the fuss of going was too much effort.

Bedtime became the worst time of the day at our house. The extra drinks and the "Mommy, I just want to tell you one more thing" left me completely flustered. How I needed Rog at 9:00 p.m.! In anger and frustration I'd demand, "You must go to sleep NOW!" They'd respond with hurt tears because I rushed them so. Putting them to bed without Rog symbolized my whole aloneness as a parent. For months I exaggerated the problem out of all proportion.

When I couldn't swing the one-parent household, I cried tears of hurt and resentment. "I just don't know how to handle this alone," I pleaded to the two wide-eyed boys before me. Usually I received the sympathy I needed and an attempt on their part to do better. I certainly don't recommend it as a tool to be used often, but I don't think it hurt them to see sometimes my honest frustrations with my total responsibility.

After a lot of stumbling and a lot of worry, by spring I finally seemed to regroup my strength as a parent and consciously determined that I could raise them alone after all. "Certainly I am creative and intelligent enough to raise two young boys," I told myself repeatedly.

Ours had been the typical family with the father's voice carrying more weight. Convincing two lively boys that I was in control required consistency and authority that my emotional condition didn't always allow. However, I managed much better once I made up my mind that I could do it. Instead of blaming and needling the boys about never getting ready on time, I learned to make a list of things that needed to be done if they wished to go along. A list of responsibilities also brought more ready cooperation with chores around the home. The bedtime battle was won by starting earlier and having a story time which settled them down. Picking fights with each other brought sitting on chairs in separate rooms no matter whose fault it was.

Grandparents, relatives, Joyce (the young teacher who moved in), and a circle of young mothers with whom I've always exchanged baby-sitting helped me in this awesome task of being an only parent. They affirmed my discipline, reminded me that all children go through difficult stages, and helped me remember that teasing and picking are as natural as rain in spring. They took care of Chad and Dereck often when I had plans or needed to get out.

# THE NEED TO BE INCLUDED

Chad and Dereck needed to be involved with other people to fill the void in their lives. How fortunate we were that grandparents, cousins, and many friends lived nearby. Yet at first the situation was disturbingly uncomfortable and being with other families was awkward.

Gathering around the table and seeing that we were missing a daddy was upsetting to everyone. Not having a man for the other husband to visit with was clumsy. I didn't especially like always riding in the backseat with the kids when we went somewhere with another family. Friendly arguments about whether my family's meal should be put on their restaurant check frustrated me. I not only hated to feel indebted but I knew the expense was considerable.

My plea to other families was, "Just stick with us! We can overcome the awkwardness if you can." I worked hard to make other couples feel comfortable in a house without a man. One night some friends and their three children dropped in. During the conversation the husband confessed that he had thought maybe just his wife and the boys should come, but that he had really enjoyed the visit too. How much we needed to be treated like a normal family!

"I'll work at it if you will," I said to those around me. Swallowing my pride, I accepted riding in the backseat. Figuring out ways of doing things in return made me feel better. I learned either to slip money quietly to the man ahead of time or gratefully accept his paying instead of grabbing for the check.

I vowed to overcome my awkwardness because I knew how much being with other families would add to my sons' lives. People helped us find some laughter in life again. Taking the kids on an outing, stopping at Farell's ice-cream parlor to celebrate a birthday, or just spending a quiet day playing games by the fire gave such relief to our sadness.

Not only were we surrounded by families who took time to care but we also made a real effort to make ourselves available. The first year, Sundays brought emotional battles that were hard to handle. It had been our family day and I just couldn't cope with coming home to an empty house. With gratitude I accepted any invitations that were extended to us or took the initative to plan activities.

Once when Dereck was lamenting that he'd never have a daddy the rest of his life, I brushed off his tears with, "I'll just have to be both mommy and daddy." With eyes wide and in a knowing voice he informed me, "Oh, *you* can't be a daddy!" Of course I knew he was right.

Chad and Dereck needed other husbands and fathers to provide the male image for them. At first both had an understandably strong attraction for men. In Dereck it was obvious. He would hug or climb on the lap of any man who paid attention to him, including sales clerks or casual visitors. Chad hid his need behind a quiet request for a game of checkers or a teasing punch at someone he knew well.

Grandfathers served as good models; the boys loved having them drop by for a game or two. It was good for Chad and Dereck to see Joyce's fiancé, George, frequently. They dropped everything and ran to the door to greet him much as they used to meet Rog when he returned from work. He tussled and teased them a bit, and they seemed satisfied.

Maynard, a good friend whose own children are older, was adopted as an uncle-type and sometime substitute dad. When he acted as Dereck's dad visiting Sunday school class on Father's Day, Dereck proudly told everyone, "My daddy is in heaven, but Maynard is here for me!" The thoughtfulness of that teacher in arranging such a happening and the kindness of many other father relatives and friends who have taken a special interest in Chad and Dereck have made their adjustment to life without a father so much easier and less lonely.

Several young wives have told me that if their husbands died, they don't know if they could count on the families in their group to stick with them. Couples with children should look about them and consider whether they are surrounded by people — friends and relatives — who would emotionally support and include their children and wife (or husband) if one of them died. Ask your friends. The answer will either bring great comfort or leave you quite shaken. Parents should make a conscious effort to have their children relate to other adults who care about them, especially if the family lives away from relatives. I pray that those who have given so much help to us will have their love returned manyfold if they are ever left alone with a family.

When I faced the awesome task of keeping up a house with only the small amount of help from the boys, I was overpowered. However, not only have we received emotional support from other families, but we have been given physical help so that we can live without a man around. My father is a great fix-it person and has given us all kinds of help, from building things for the boys to wiring lights. People have seeded the lawn, chopped wood, cleaned up fallen brush, supplied chips for the flower beds, wire-meshed our eave spouts, repaired machinery, and moved heavy things. They've built a large swing set, structured a giant sandbox, and repaired bicycles. One friend whom I trusted took me under his business wing and helped make financial decisions when I didn't feel up to it.

Recovery from crippling sadness was made easier for us by people who were willing to become involved with us as a family!

# FACING
# A COUPLED SOCIETY

A good many of my coping problems involved the emotional frustration of fitting into a couple-oriented society. I wasn't married anymore, but I certainly wasn't single either. Unfortunately, there's such a definite division between the two that I foolishly thought I had to be on one side or the other! I wasted a lot of energy worrying about where I belonged. Would my married friends still be with me in a year or would I have to find new single ones?

The whole thing crystalized with frightening clarity during an evening of conversation with friends. The wife talked at length about the housecleaning, the baking, and the bustle of getting ready for holiday company. Although I had loved planning and entertaining, her concerns sounded completely foreign to me — as if I had never been there and would never be there again. It all seemed vague and part of being a couple. I sat completely empty and dazed by the knowledge of how my life had changed.

How things had changed! The mechanics of fitting into society alone are just plain awkward. Going unescorted into group meetings, facing embarrassing seating arrangements at dinner parties, and paying the bill when eating out made me want to give up. At first facing a group of all couples made me want to run home to my seclusion.

My friends were persistent in making me feel comfortable. Four weeks after Rog died, I attended my first party — a farewell for friends moving to another state. Those invited were members of our study group and husbands — all people I knew well. The planned activity was loosely structured and noncoupled. Although there was obviously someone missing, I enjoyed the night and thanked God I had friends who could be so sensitive.

I thanked God often during those bad months as couples included me in parties, took me to plays and concerts, and asked me out for dinner. Often I breathed a prayer of gratitude that both the wife and the husband of many of the couples were my personal friends. I felt they both wanted me along; the husband wasn't just enduring or they weren't including me out of a sense of duty. When inviting me they used words like, "We want you," not "We haven't done much for you so we thought we'd take you to —" Some of the husbands learned to escort two ladies with real style, which minimized the tagalong feeling. A few good social experiences made up for the bad, awkward times when I felt completely out of it.

Simply to say I had super people surrounding me doesn't communicate the many ways they emotionally helped me cope with a coupled society. I have the kind of friends who at parties or restaurant dinners often choose to sit by the person with whom they haven't conversed for a while. They don't stay glued together as couples, nor do the men congregate separately.

I needed to be with men and women. I enjoyed male conversation as much as I did before and would have been utterly bored if I had been limited to a world of only women. Our married life meant being with people and doing a lot of interesting things. To have all of that cut off suddenly would have been more than I could endure.

Yet widow after widow told me of the exclusion they experienced. Couples simply stopped inviting them. "When I heard the group got together without me, I cried for days," or "We always celebrated our birthdays together; I didn't even get a phone call from them," and

"When Bob died, the only couples that cared about me were relatives," are the kinds of statements hurting widows have shared. Good friends suddenly were awkwardly absent. If the wives kept up the friendship, it usually meant coming without the husband. Someone would call and say, "I'd like to come over tonight. My husband is out of town."

Perhaps such couples could hide behind the excuse, "We really didn't know what to do so we wouldn't hurt her feelings, so we just didn't do anything." Or, "We thought it would be too awkward and she'd just miss her husband more if she'd be with couples."

Believe me, the painful experience of missing Rog and being reminded of him when I was with other couples was not as hurtful as adding exclusion to loss. Death can't be helped; exclusion can — and it's like a slap in the face of an already broken person. Of such insensitive couples, those of us alone almost maliciously think, "Just wait till they face living alone!"

Awkwardness can be handled with a little planning. Much uneasiness can be eliminated by making sure the person alone has someone with whom to sit and by structuring the activity so that it isn't all partner-centered. Names of groups can be very limiting. Instead of talking about the "married fellowship" one church changed the name to "adult fellowship."

I wanted to choose the things I could handle, not have others decide for me. I didn't want people just to assume I wouldn't want to come.

During the first year I wasn't ready to go some places or be in a couples' Bible study group, but I was invited and given the choice and that felt good.

Including the widowed, who seem to be emotionally at sea, involves risk. There's no assurance that the fun and good times of the evening won't suddenly seem empty and trite to us. There's no guarantee that in spite of all the careful planning, we won't be hurt or have an awful time. There will be awkward times such as the sickening silence which filled the room when a man, raving about not being able to sleep if his wife wasn't in bed with with him, remembered that I was standing there. It takes a sense of humor from everyone.

I wanted people to be natural around me. I wanted a husband and wife to touch each other and show affection if that was part of their personality as a couple. It might remind me that I was alone, but it hurt more to think that my presence made couples stiff and unnatural. I didn't like being considered a walking face of death which said, "One day you too will be alone!"

At first I didn't have much energy to return friendship. Any feeling of coldness and awkwardness made me want to withdraw because I took it as personal rejection. However, as the months continued, I knew that I couldn't always expect others to bend over backward to make me feel comfortable. If I wanted to continue to be involved with people, I needed to try hard! Although I expected my friends to accept my swings in moods and not to make me feel guilty when life didn't seem very bright, I knew that I couldn't remain long-faced or dazed-beyond-caring if I wanted to be included.

Whenever I talk about including others, people tell me that they've tried. "After John lost his wife, we continued to invite him to our parties, but he spent the whole evening talking about the second coming of Christ and being united with his wife. After he ruined several evenings, all the hostesses were afraid to invite him," they tell me, or, "She is so completely absorbed in her problems that she will corner anyone she can and go on and on. She has spoiled so many fun evenings."

Maybe it did mean forcing myself to be sociable or feigning interest at times. Sometimes it meant smothering the desire to talk about Rog or about death. Often it meant battling my feelings of being different or trying to pull myself out of a bad mood before anyone noticed.

Sometimes I didn't feel like being with couples and wished for a group of people who could understand my feelings and wanted to talk about the same things I did. I felt there should be some kind of effort or organization to help me, and perhaps a lifeline for other people going through grief who did not find the kind of support that I had. I'm very much opposed to the widowed withdrawing from coupled society and finding all their fellowship in isolated cliques who "understand." However, I needed the empathy of a few friends who had also lost mates.

One of the biggest problems I had with our couple-structured society was the definite impression it gave me that remarriage should be my ultimate goal. Whether real or imagined, I often felt treated as if I were in a temporary state waiting for that right person to come along so I could be a normal person again. By the eighth month I heard, "If you can just endure this period, you'll marry again someday." After all I had already been through, the enduring of which they spoke sounded awful! Horrified I thought, "This can't be for me!"

Seeing widowed people pressured into unsatisfactory marriages simply because they couldn't cope with a coupled society frightened me. Don't make me feel I'd better marry soon if I want to remain a part of things. There are enough personal pressures that leave me vulnerable without society making remarriage necessary as my ticket back into life.

# DEVOURED
# BY DEATH

By the end of the ninth month I was totally exhausted and tired of having been devoured by grief. Living with death had been like wearing discolored glasses or like having a film over my eyes. It had altered my whole pattern of thinking. No decision, no activity, and no work had been faced without regard to what had happened to me. Even when I was having a good time, it was there. The fact that I had lost my husband hovered over every conversation and every relationship. I hated meeting new people;

I felt I had to tell them about Rog. Seeing casual acquaintances who already knew my circumstances resulted in conversations that just hung there.

There had been no forgetting it. For such a long time I felt like a walking zombie with a big sign. "I Lost My Husband," hung on my back. Organized discussion groups such as Sunday school classes and study groups had a horribly unsettling effect. I felt that I put a strain on any group I was in, providing an obvious reminder that all problems or concerns seem minor compared with the death crisis. My presence, I felt, stifled open sharing.

I hadn't wanted to cry, so I left many groups emotionally exhausted from bottling up my feelings. At first I just couldn't share with groups my pain of coping. I could open up to one or several friends at a time, but put them all together in a study group or a class situation and I felt intimidated about sharing anything negative.

At first I was too tired to take the risk. And I wasn't sure if I could trust people to understand that, in spite of being a Christian, I had to struggle with all kinds of coping problems. I wasn't sure I wanted them to know how painful was the road I walked — how it had been consuming me and how near it came to defeating me at times.

The public faces I wore were not always true faces, but at the time seemed necessary for survival in society. I'm glad I had a few close friends who heard and helped so that I didn't need to corner people with my problems or spill my emotions in groups. I'm not sure I could have stood the world seeing behind all my faces. Yet, once I stopped trying to be strong, I started finding hints of healing.

Perhaps if I had opened up sooner, I would have stood up better against the devouring nature of death. In March, when I consented to do a little sharing with groups and some writing, I was gratified by the way people not only withheld criticism but identified with my feelings. However, sharing is a risk. It was much easier to let everyone think I'd "done so well" than to trust them with my struggles.

Yes, death had consumed me for many months. It was like losing my innocence. The happy expectations and all-is-well zeal on which I had structured my life were gone. I felt cheated out of all the feelings of well-being that had characterized my life. I hated the thought of trying to live peacefully with unhappiness, but felt it was probably the best I could do.

At times a nagging fear that I might lose the boys, too, or that they might get the disease gripped my insides. I often lamented, "If I could just know that they would grow to be healthy, useful adults, I'd be content." Not wanting to convey my fear to them, I tried hard not to be overprotective.

But periodically fear clutched me hard. Death had always happened "out there." Suddenly, it seemed to be all around me. Our minister's twenty-eight-year old son, a medical student, drowned while fishing a month after we had buried Rog. Not only did they have to go through three weeks of agonizing search till they found his body, but their six-month-old granddaughter died of spinal meningitis at the same time. Seeing death hit twice in the same family greatly increased my own anxiety. Could I face another death in the family?

Six months later I watched a friend, Lois, who had been so kind to me, succumb to cancer. She had sent me a note in February from Nicaragua where she was touring with her family; by April she was dead. The knowledge that death can sneak up quickly troubled me deeply. What would happen to the boys if I died suddenly?

Recently we buried my good aunt, who had given me a book which helped pull me toward some new goals. She had told me how much Rog's optimistic view of his illness had meant to her when she had days of pain. "I never even knew he was weak. That's how I want to bear my pain," she had said. She must have covered well, because she died three weeks after surgery revealed she had cancer. Her funeral reminded me how weary of death I had become!

In my low moments, I sat and shuddered. Who would be next? I became painfully aware that the more people I love, the more are my chances of being hurt by death. If I continue to live, I'll see more separation and more pain. Loving is such risky business!

In my good moments, I knew in my heart that death's tough lesson was being seared there with irons of wisdom. Death, more than anything else, sharply points up the necessity of grasping each moment of life and living it as fully as possible while we may. Death was making me intensely aware of the importance of good relationships and was bringing into sharper focus those things in life which I considered valuable.

Throughout the year after Rog died, I kept asking myself, "Will I ever really be happy again? Will I ever deeply believe again that life is fulfilling, that it is to be lived with energy and purpose?" I was so tired of thinking about death. I wanted desperately to return to normalcy. Yet it seemed I was always reaching backwards and couldn't quite leave behind my crushed dreams. Perhaps I felt a kind of security in my suffering and was fearful about moving ahead to an unknown future.

The point of escape from the exhausting hold of grief comes at different times for people. Some are ready to grasp life again within months; some fight a much longer battle which lasts for years. To compare ourselves and feel guilty that we aren't coping as well as the next person simply compounds the problem. If during one of my tough times I'd hear the words, "Sue Ann is doing so well since the death," I either became defensive and felt it was a slam in my face saying, "Why aren't you?" or I wanted to laugh and say, "It could be a mask. I know all about putting up a front."

For me it took nearly a year before I was ready to take the risks and make the necessary effort to escape the clutches of sorrow. I was not only tired of being suppressed by grief, but I was determined, whatever it took, to pull myself out from under its load and think about life again. In my exhaustion with death, would I take a sane road? What would I do to overcome the suffocation of grief?

# HOW
# WOULD I ESCAPE?

How could I ever forget what had happened?
How could I escape the heaviness? Would I
make some crazy mistakes in my attempt to get
away from the insufferable strain caused by
death?

I don't like pain! Although I know a person
is supposed to develop real character by suffering, I would much rather have learned my
lessons in a less dreadful way. As I faced
aching grief, I hoped for a panacea, a simple
cure, that would take away the pain. I'm very

much a product of a society which tells me that there's a pill, an escape, for every ailment. There had to be something somewhere to take away the hurt!

For a time I thought I couldn't stand to live in Archbold any longer. Our house was a sanctuary, but the community seemed a cage. Everyone knew me. Everywhere I went I faced activity and people who reminded me that Rog wasn't here. I thought that a new town, a new environment, and even new friends might help me forget.

But I had nowhere I wanted to go. I knew I couldn't just pick up and move the boys to a strange community. It was also clear that I wasn't ready to face the pressure of meeting new people and of being away from relatives and friends who were helping me so much.

I can't recall all the muddled ways of escape that played on my mind. At one point I thought that I could become a great writer as Catherine Marshall did after her husband's death. Then when I was famous, it wouldn't hurt so much that I didn't have Rog. I thought maybe I should use the insurance money and take a glamorous world tour. We had loved to travel. Maybe in the Swiss mountains I could forget about the empty house in Ohio. It crossed my mind that I should go on weekend visits and attend all kinds of meetings in other communities because I just might meet a charming knight and all my pain would vanish!

The advice to make few major decisions

the first year is sometimes hard to follow. I read and heard about widows who had sold their homes in haste and later regretted it, widows who were taken advantage of when quickly selling assets or stock, widows who quickly spent all the insurance money, and those who grabbed the first man who came along.

I was determined not to allow the "craziness of grief" to cause me to make foolish decisions. Those of us wrestling with sorrow need the tolerance of others. We are often not ourselves. If you haven't included us with your families and given us the strong emotional support we need to feel confident so that we can make sane choices, then you scarcely have a right to be judgmental if we make mistakes.

To "take one day at a time" can be a cheap cliché thrown from mouths who have not known the cracking bitterness of grief. But it can also be advice which, when lived, becomes profoundly meaningful. I could resolve to cope with my grief and decide to make it a good day by sheer mental and emotional fortitude if I broke time into small segments. It was when I looked ahead too far and thought of one year, or ten years, without Rog that the pain was most unbearable.

The summer, which had always been special for us, loomed large before me. Summer had always spelled VACATION in big letters. It meant packing the camper for weekends by a lake and enjoying picnics on the patio with other families. It usually meant taking a longer

trip of some kind. With the coming of March,
I knew that I had made it through the winter
months. I had managed a kind of semihiberna-
tion which included a lot of reading and medi-
tation along with a little writing, but I didn't
see how I could face the summer alone.

I tried desperately to think of someplace
we could go for those three months. I tried to
get a position at a summer camp and was told,
"We can't use someone with two children,
expecially if you're alone." The letter I was
going to send to our church mission board to
volunteer for some kind of service is still in
the drawer. What could I do with two small
children, and where could I go so that they
would have a good summer? Friends coun-
seled me just to sit tight. "You may feel differently later," they said.

By May I did feel differently. I had smothered my selfish desire to get away so that I could
forget our past summers and had resolved to
make it a happy summer for Chad and Dereck.
The camper had to be sold. I knew I couldn't
vacation with a camper by myself. As they
pulled the camper away, I heard Dereck sobbing, "We'll never have any fun without
Daddy. I know we won't!" I pulled him close
to me and vowed that I would do all I could to
make summer fun.

We could accept invitations to go on weekend
trips or go camping with other families. We could
spend a week at the lake with my sister and
her family. And we could enjoy just being in
our community. Chad took lessons and became

a good swimmer; so at least three afternoons a week we swam together. He played Pee Wee baseball and enjoyed getting to know all the kids in our development. Dereck conquered a two-wheeled bicycle and learned to duck his head at the pool. Our backyard is wooded and private so it was almost like camping. By summer I was enjoying our new house again and started to work on some decorating ideas which had stopped completely when Rog died.

Although escape in some form is sometimes necessary and can act as a safety valve, it was good to know I could work through my grief right in my own backyard. The possibilities for evasive, impulsive, and sometimes tragic ways of forgetting are very real.

# GRABBING
# FOR HAPPINESS

Grief left me with many of the symptoms that waiting always had — with unsettled stomach, restlessness, and why-can't-it-be-over type of questions. I felt suspended in time! Everything seemed so uncertain.

I went through a period when all my plans seemed uprooted. What kind of life could I count on for the future? Before there had never been enough time for all the things I hoped to do. Now I wasn't even sure what I wanted to do.

I only knew I wanted to be happy and that I

had a haunting desire to return to normal. Happiness became "the big red apple." I knew that by craving it too much, I was opening myself to the temptation of grabbing for anything to make me happy. Although I knew better, for a time it seemed I was just sitting and waiting for happiness to come to me. Joy had to be around the next bend. It was tempting to think, "By next month, by next year I'll surely have found happiness again."

I've always known that joy and peace come from within, that happiness is a by-product and not a goal to be pursued in itself. I had always agreed with the poster on Rog's office wall which said, "Happiness is like a butterfly. The more you chase it, the more it will elude you." But now I found myself tempted to do some grabbing and some chasing.

One of the most tempting solutions to unhappiness was to follow the advice of several friends and become totally immersed in a career. One friend coped with her divorce by becoming so busy she couldn't think. She worked as many hours and as many weekends as possible to avoid facing herself.

Physical strain can be good for grief. Wearing off frustration is a valid reason for being involved and busy. I spent too much time reading, thinking, and working things out in my mind and didn't balance it with enough physical activity. My body felt much older and at times I felt weak. I was out of shape. I see now that emotional and physical health go together.

Being needed and feeling that one is doing

something worthwhile are important in healing grief. The working woman with an interesting job to involve herself has a natural diversion from too much concentration on grief. When I was a high school girl who received the advice that I should prepare for a career "in case something happens to your husband," my feathers ruffled a bit. That certainly wasn't why I wanted a degree. Yet, how fortunate I am to have training in a profession I really enjoy. My heart cries for women who wanted to be full-time mothers and housewives but suddenly are forced to support themselves at a job they neither like nor wanted.

Yet there seems to be something so artificial about deliberately becoming busy to escape one's grief. By looking too soon for a new job to solve my problems, I would have only added more frustration. I wanted to return to the classroom when I had a desire to teach, not just as a means of escaping and forgetting. I'm glad I didn't let others push me into involvement that I wasn't ready to handle. I knew I was the one who would have to live with the hectic schedule and the demands of the job. Just being busy is not always the same as being happy.

For the widowed mother, a second temptation is to submerge herself completely in the lives of her children. In areas where I depended on Rog too heavily for some sort of identity, I could now be looking to the children for that fulfillment. Expectations could run unreasonably high if I devoted myself exclusively to their success. If I had expected my husband to make me "somebody," I would now expect the boys to take on that responsibility.

I loved Chad and Dereck so strongly that I thought about devoting myself wholly to their well-being. With doting-mother feelings, I was tempted to say, "I'll draw my happiness through dedication to my sons." I found myself beginning to cling to them as "all I had left," and found myself becoming overprotective and more demanding of their love. Overconcern for the children was stifling them and leaving me empty as well. I realized that if I depend *only* on the boys to make me happy, I'll again face a traumatic experience when they become old enough to leave home.

When happiness is viewed as something to grab, the widow who has once known a good marriage relationship faces a lot of internal pressure suggesting that remarriage would be the answer to her frustrations. To love again would, more than anything else, quickly bring the return to normalcy for which we long.

I went through three basic stages in my view of remarriage. The first six months I felt so tied to Rog that I couldn't imagine remarriage. No one could ever take his place, I was sure. The boys' hope for a new daddy crushed me. When friends said quietly, "You'll love again sometime," I thought they couldn't possibly understand the way I still loved Rog. "No," I thought, "I'll make it alone. We will thank God that we had Rog for those good years and live in the memory of that love."

Funny thing though — memories don't help take care of the kids, listen to my conversation, or fill the house with fun. By the seventh and eighth months I could hardly cope with my loneliness for Rog, the empty house, and the being alone. I panicked with the realization that if I couldn't have Rog, I'd have to find a substitute.

The second stage came hard and painfully, causing a lot of conflict as I continually argued with myself about the pros and cons of remarriage. It was a time when I thought I could use someone to help me forget. I was tempted to feel that anything might be better than being alone. I thought I was a sensible person and I had told my friends to make sure I didn't make a bad mistake. Yet if I had learned to know someone with the same grief experience, I might have been persuaded, however reluctantly, to grab onto a new marriage to escape. How sad it would have been to discover later that I had married because of a grief need or in sympathy for the man. To find out that our sadness was all we had in common would have been an unendurable disappointment. I knew I was too young to settle for that kind of marriage. I needed more than grief companionship. I often pleaded with God to protect me from being pressured into an unsatisfactory relationship.

When responsibilities with the children overwhelmed me, I helplessly felt like advertising, "Needed: One good father for two lively boys." Rationally, I knew that remarriage does not always bring the father relationship for the children that was expected. At that point, I would have constantly measured any man against the kind of father Rog had been. As a mother I agreed with those who said the boys should have a father, but as a woman in society I could not actively seek out a man who would make a good daddy. Besides, I told myself that I would never marry someone just to provide a male influence for the boys.

Sometimes I turned cold with the feeling that I needed a man to fill the void. For as long as I could remember, there had always been some special guy in my life. After nine years of marriage to Rog who had given me so much love and attention, I realized how very much it meant to have a special man to care for me alone! I cherished the affection and warmth of love and felt something precious was missing from my life. Also, the coupled society nearly convinces a woman that she is incomplete, an empty, shapeless vessel waiting to be filled with love — not whole until loved of man. Countering society's preoccupation with sexual fulfillment and my memories of being loved and accepted made being alone very difficult. Feeling like half a person left me very vulnerable. I knew this and it scared me. I could only hope that by understanding my situation, I could remain rational and not be swept away by emotions.

Whenever Rog and I had discussed death, Rog always saw remarriage as a good thing — a sign that the first marriage had been pleasing.

Although I always laughingly tried to make him promise to mourn my death for a year if I went first, I basically agreed with him.

When I was finally ready to acknowledge that I was strong enough to get to know someone and that dating could possibly be a good thing, I fell flat with the realization that at age thirty the field of available men seems utterly barren. I seemed either too old or too young! There were few thirtyish singles left. There were numbers of men who had learned the heartbreak of a broken relationship, but getting entangled in a divorce situation seemed threatening. Widows in America outnumber widowers four to one. For the widow my age the ratio has to be even more staggering.

When I realistically faced the odds against readily meeting someone with whom I would want to tie my life, I knew that I could not sit around waiting for marriage to rescue me! I gradually and confidently moved into the third state, where I said, "Yes, remarriage could add meaning and beauty to my life. But an unwise, grabbed-for marriage would be completely awful. With this conviction, I knew that I was not lonely or unhappy enough to settle for a Band-Aid marriage.

Being included in social activities and having male as well as female friends who told me I was an attractive, valuable person, loved for being myself, and not just as part of a couple, gave me confidence. As more and more people treated me as an individual, I gradually stopped viewing myself as the poor, incomplete widow.

Being alone had cruelly wiped away so much of my self-assurance that I really needed people who affirmed me and encouraged me to rebuild my life as an independent person — able to live securely alone, open to love again, but not clutching for a man as survival.

With courage I came to the point where I no longer viewed marriage as a necessity for fulfillment. During this third stage, I probably overreacted by feeling that I had to prove my self-sufficiency. I overcompensated in other areas to prove I was a "whole" person. However, I'm glad I had time to work through my grief, time to gain the security of making it alone — without the prospect of another husband waiting in the wings "to save me." If I love again, marriage will come for itself, not as an escape.

Crutches wear out quickly. Heavy immersion in a career, possessive motherhood, and a remarriage grabbed in panic would have been crutches for me. When I lean too hard I often fall!

# QUIET
# HEALING

Recovery didn't come in any observable way. There wasn't any sudden healing or release from sorrow. Instead it was a kind of quietness that began unaware.

The knowledge that my days didn't have to be a waiting experience came steadily and with growing power. With surprise I realized that I was no longer *always* forcing myself to enjoy life. I was beginning to care about the present — perhaps starting to revive.

The gritting-my-teeth kind of coping that had

helped me through the many low times of that first year of grief gradually was replaced with a "Yes, I think life can be good again" way of coping.

My emotions fluctuated less often now and when the depression or pessimism did come, the depth of the fall seemed minor compared to where I had been a year ago. Thanksgiving and Christmas the second time around still seemed empty without Rog, but I didn't have to force myself to be busy to enjoy the holidays. Gone was the guilt over my weakness. I could increasingly see that working through my overwhelming and defeating problems brought stronger emotional health than could any kind of escaping, ignoring, or waiting for time to heal.

The heavy pain had been shed unaware sometime during the fun of the bright summer. There were still days when my stomach tightened with the hurt which came flooding back, and I could hardly stand it that Rog wasn't present to share some happening with us. But the ache was less crushing.

Worry about being an only-parent could still be triggered easily by hard-to-handle situations with the children, but the panic was gone. I found myself relaxing and more frequently avoiding the stress of needing to show people that I was doing a good job as a single parent. Uncomfortable social experiences continued, but I was finding myself surprisingly less awkward as a person alone in society than I had thought possible. My friends were still with me a year later and I was abundantly included.

I was no longer always exhausted from concentration on death. My mind was becoming filled with other thoughts. Even though I continued to keep a fairly loose schedule and still had problems planning ahead and committing myself to detail, I learned that entertaining alone could be good. Getting involved in community activity could be worthwhile. I found serving on a committee to plan activities and recruit volunteers for a local museum village a challenge.

In spite of the fact that I affirmed myself for my ability to discuss death and look it in the face no longer as a foreboding stranger, the whole harsh reality of separation could come thundering back, especially on dark days or during funerals of other people. (Just because I was working through one death, I could not predict what my reactions would be the next time I faced a painful loss!)

The temptation to chase happiness became less powerful as I looked more inward and upward for answers. I began to see that quietness of soul and inward peace were more important than an elusive happiness. The whole process of healing finally seemed to be slowly coming together when I started to see myself as a whole person instead of half of the couple that no longer existed. When I realized with growing confidence that there were still a lot of possibilities open to me, I began to be restored.

Giving up the dreams I had shared with Rog seemed so impossibly hard, so intolerably sad.

But I knew that only by stopping the past from overwhelming the present could I have any hope for the future. My love for Rog and the beautiful memories will always be a special part of my life. The deep feelings that have turned to memories are there to recall and to build upon. But the past must be kept in its proper perspective — not an obsession, not a bondage — a good thing, but not the only thing.

When I saw some other goals emerging from the cloudy blackness of a nothing-future, life slowly revived. A person can cope with meaninglessness for only so long. Our only hope, when things happen that cannot be changed, is to find and develop other reasons for living. When our dreams are shattered beyond repair, our best salvation is to pray for and eventually dream *possible* dreams, to leave behind our wishes and our "if onlys" and find some purpose to give meaning to life.

If you're a widow going through the blackness of despair, I know you can't even think about goals. It requires too much effort. Be kind to yourself! You have reason to cry, to be adrift, and to go through the long process of grief.

Don't rush into forming new goals, but if there's something you've wanted to do, some talent you'd like to develop, or some interest that is ever so slight, hold to it. Use any spark of life you can find — anything that will give you a feeling of self-worth and self-wholeness that doesn't depend on your past or on your imaginary future. To married women

I say, love your husband completely but realize that you are a person without him. Share life but have a personal identity along with your identity as a couple.

The study group I attended concerned itself with developing the God-given gifts which are too often hidden deeply within. We acknowledged and called forth each other's talents and experiences and helped mesh them with the needs we saw around us. One week we each imagined all the things we would *like* to do if we could. Before Rog died my list would have been long. After a hopeless year of grief when I wanted to do nothing except be the wife that was no longer possible, I found my list growing again. I reclaimed the awareness that I had many things for which to hope.

I could search for wisdom. Not a pious pie-in-the-sky sort of truth, and not only an intellectual understanding, but a real kind of knowing what is right and good and best. I'd like to be able to discern the mysteries of life and of death and flow with them. I'd like to perceive this life as part of eternity and be concerned with the idea of adding life to my years instead of stumbling along with the hope of just adding years to my life.

At the top of my list was the desire to be a good mother. How fantastically rewarding it would be to have the boys look back to their childhood and say, "In spite of the death of our father, we had a warm, accepting, and stimulating home."

Of course, bad times with the children are still with me. Mothering means facing a lot of hassles. But mothering also means Dereck cuddling in my arms with a kiss and an "I love you, Mommy" or a jubilant arrival home from nursery class with a "Hi, Mom, I had a good time." It means receiving a stool that Chad made on his new workbench, listening to riddles of a second-grader, or receiving the largest and prettiest Mother's Day card. It means hearing reports that your children are well-behaved, fun-to-have-around youngsters, and watching Chad and Dereck play together in quiet harmony for hours.

Being a mother — even alone — can make life full and happy. A good day came when I stopped blaming all our problems on Rog's death and decided that I wasn't doing so badly by myself. How good I feel when I'm confident that I can raise the boys.

In September, one year after Rog died, I taught a speech course for several hours a week at a local technical college and led an adult education class one night a week. I enjoyed being back in the classroom. After five years away from it, I realized anew that a teaching career would again be fulfilling. That knowledge has given me a great deal of security.

By fall I started receiving invitations to share my walk through grief with many groups. Although talking about death and its realities is always an emotionally draining experience, the new understanding that I see on the faces of the audience makes the strain worthwhile.

Lecturing has given me the opportunity to share with many interesting people. I've learned a lot!

The highest plateau of healing that I've discovered so far (and I'm sure I'll move on) is the actual turning of tragedy and suffering into some good. I could shrug it off as a quirk in my work-ethic, serious-view-of-life heritage which says, "Janette, your hope comes by serving others." Or I can call upon my interpretation of Romans 8:28, "All things work together for good to them that love God," which says to me, "God gives strength to us to make good out of bad." I don't see a God on His throne snapping out decisions and pushing me through doors of His will, but I do see God helping me make choices in accord with His desire for my harmony with Him. The most understandable reason for turning tragedy around is simply that it feels good!

Perhaps it is enough to know I have learned death's tough lessons concerning the unmeasured value of living life fully and the unequaled worth of caring human relationships. It's satisfying to know that I depend less on my outward surroundings and circumstances for my peace. It's tempting to think of this "making something good" only in a personal way — if my life is happy again that is enough.

Yet it seems that my terrifying walk through grief brought an experience that should be shared, an awareness of the needs of the widowed which must be taken seriously. I envisioned starting a group — a kind of visible, helping hand extended to people facing the death crisis. Upset by the lonely hearts tone or the kind of advice that some groups give the person in grief, I felt there should be some type of religious organization available to give realistic counsel and emotional support. There should be a group for sharing and for educating people to cope with death.

By chance I read the book, *After the Flowers Have Gone*, which is the story of Bea Decker, a widow who felt this same need. She determined to start a religious, nondenominational organization to help others. The effort became known as THEOS,° an acronym for They Help Each Other Spiritually, and also appropriately the Greek word for God. Monthly meetings evolved. A monthly publication, which carries program information and interesting related articles, is sent to any widowed person on request. Each spring and fall people who have lost a partner are invited to a retreat where they can share and hear ideas of ways to adjust.

People who have journeyed the valley helping other people see some light at the end of the tunnel — that sounds good! The widowed in deep grief need to be told by someone who has experienced the great hurt, "Yes, you will sleep well again, your food will taste good again, you will laugh, find work satisfying, and share real joy with your children." If you

---

°THEOS Foundation, 11609 Frankstown Road, Pittsburgh, Pennsylvania 15235.

feel that you or someone dear to you needs the kind of empathy — not sympathy — that such a group can give, perhaps you can relate to this organization or extend a similar kind of helping hand of your own in your area.

This in no way minimizes the importance of personal involvement with friends and relatives whose surrounding love is so desperately needed. The walk through grief cannot be made without help. It may seem that someone has done well alone, but often the grief has simply been suppressed to fester and boil over years later. The support, the listening, and the including have to be there! The widowed need others to be God's gift to their need!

Fifteen months after the death that so changed my life, as I write this, not all my problems have been solved and recovery is not complete. I'm not clicking my heels with happiness (that kind of abandoned joy may be a state of innocence which can never entirely return). But I am again living with quiet, unreserved pleasure, knowing that I have not been defeated by my slow, hard walk through grief.

**Janette (Rupp) Klopfenstein** was born at Pettisville, Ohio, and lives at nearby Archbold. She graduated from the Pettisville High School, attended Goshen College, Goshen, Indiana, and received her BA degree in Comprehensive Language Arts from Defiance College, Defiance Ohio.

Janette has taught at Wauseon High School and at Northwest Technical College in her hometown. Besides being mother to her sons, Chad and Dereck, she has been involved in public speaking and community and church projects.

Although this is Janette's first book, her articles have appeared in *Christian Living*, *Gospel Herald*, and *The Director*.